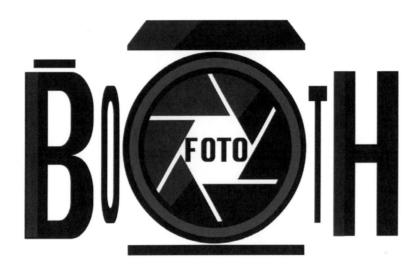

This book is dedicated to my
Uncle John.

Social Media & Contact

 www.shutter-fotos.ca

 elyse@shutter-fotos.ca

 @shutter_fotos

 @ShutterFotos

 @FotoBoothphotography

About the Author

Elyse Booth is an international photographer and educator. She has travelled around the world photographing nature, people, culture, architectural icons, animals and lifestyle content. A few of the places she has travelled to include: Hawaii, Iceland, Thailand, Cambodia, Malaysia, Laos, Italy, France, Ireland, Croatia, Hungary, Czech Republic, England, Scotland, Costa Rica, Bermuda and Mexico.

Elyse is an award winning Google trusted photographer. She builds virtual tours for Google Maps through her business Shutter Fotos, www.shutter-fotos.ca. Elyse has been recognized as a top performer for Google and top five in North America for her tours.

Elyse has a passion for lifelong learning. In addition to her love for travel and photography, she teaches Communications Technology in the private and public educational systems.

CPSIA information can be obtained
at www.ICGtesting.com
Printed in the USA
BVRC100529061221
623315BV00008B/184